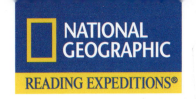

STAND UP AND SPEAK OUT

Divided Loyalties

The Barton Family During the American Revolution

By Gare Thompson
Illustrated by Barbara Kiwak

Picture Credits
4 © Owen Franken/Corbis; 5 Mapping
Specialists, Ltd.; 53 The Granger Collection,
New York; 54 (top and bottom) The Granger
Collection, New York; 56 (top) © Corbis;
(bottom left and right) National Portrait
Gallery, Smithsonian Institution/Art Resource

Produced through the worldwide resources of
the National Geographic Society, John M.
Fahey, Jr., President and Chief Executive
Officer; Gilbert M. Grosvenor, Chairman of the
Board; Nina D. Hoffman, Executive Vice
President and President, Books and Education
Publishing Group.

**Prepared by National Geographic
School Publishing**
Ericka Markman, Senior Vice President and
President, Children's Books and Education
Publishing Group; Steve Mico, Senior Vice
President, Publisher, Editorial Director; Francis
Downey, Executive Editor; Richard Easby,
Editorial Manager; Bea Jackson, Director of
Design; Cindy Olson, Art Director; Margaret
Sidlosky, Director of Illustrations; Matt
Wascavage, Manager of Publishing Services;
Lisa Pergolizzi, Sean Philpotts, Production
Managers, Ted Tucker, Production Specialist.

Manufacturing and Quality Control
Christopher A. Liedel, Chief Financial Officer;
Phillip L. Schlosser, Director; Clifton M. Brown,
Manager.

Editors
Barbara Seeber, Mary Anne Wengel

Book Development
Morrison BookWorks LLC

Book Design
Steven Curtis Design

Art Direction
Dan Banks, Project Design Company

Published by the National Geographic Society
1145 17th Street, N.W.
Washington, D.C. 20036-4688

ISBN-13: 978-0-7922-5867-4

2010 2009 2008
   3 4 5 6 7 8 9 10 11 12 13 14 15

Contents

Colonies or Country?

Before it became a country, America was made up of thirteen colonies. These colonies were ruled by Great Britain. The colonists followed British laws and paid British taxes. They were also citizens of Great Britain. But they could not vote in the British government. Some colonists, called Patriots, felt that this was unfair. The Patriots wanted to set up their own government with their own laws. Other colonists, called Loyalists, were proud to be part of Great Britain. In the 1770s, Burlington, New Jersey, was caught up in these questions of loyalty. There and elsewhere, the conflict between Patriots and Loyalists divided friends and families.

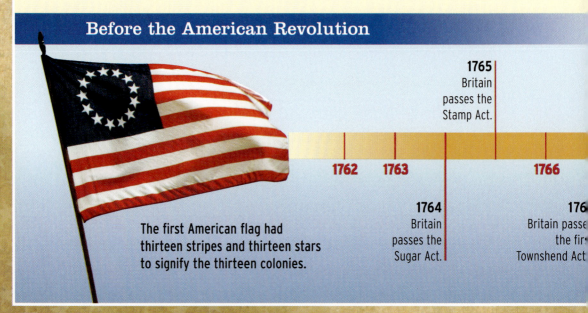

Before the American Revolution

The first American flag had thirteen stripes and thirteen stars to signify the thirteen colonies.

1762

1763

1764
Britain passes the Sugar Act.

1765
Britain passes the Stamp Act.

1766

176
Britain passe the fir Townshend Act

New Jersey and Surrounding Colonies, 1700s

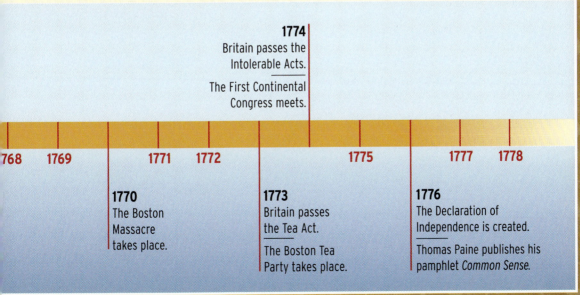

1774
Britain passes the
Intolerable Acts.

The First Continental
Congress meets.

768 1769 1771 1772 1775 1777 1778

1770
The Boston
Massacre
takes place.

1773
Britain passes
the Tea Act.

The Boston Tea
Party takes place.

1776
The Declaration of
Independence is created.

Thomas Paine publishes his
pamphlet *Common Sense*.

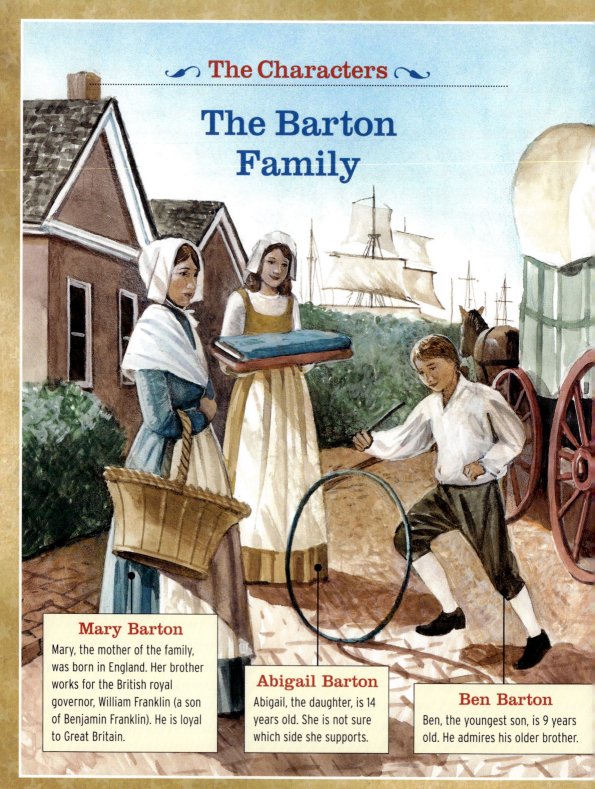

The Barton Family

Mary Barton
Mary, the mother of the family, was born in England. Her brother works for the British royal governor, William Franklin (a son of Benjamin Franklin). He is loyal to Great Britain.

Abigail Barton
Abigail, the daughter, is 14 years old. She is not sure which side she supports.

Ben Barton
Ben, the youngest son, is 9 years old. He admires his older brother.

Robert Barton

Robert, the father of the family, is a successful merchant. He depends on trading American and British goods to make a living in the family store. His loyalty is to Great Britain.

William Barton

William, the oldest son, is 17 years old. He has been attending a local school. He believes the colonies should become an independent country.

Other Characters

Narrator
Mrs. Smith
Mr. Lawson
Soldier
Customer
Crowd Members 1–5
Shopkeepers 1 and 2

 Act I

The Setting

Burlington, New Jersey, 1774-1775

Scene 1

In the Bartons' home

Narrator: Burlington, New Jersey, is alive with activity. The seeds of the American Revolution have been sown. Many in Burlington are Loyalists, but support for the Patriots is growing stronger. Farmers, shopkeepers, and others feel that they are being taxed on too many goods. They also feel that they have no say in the laws that are passed in Great Britain. The people of Burlington often hear what is happening in other colonial cities, such as New York, Boston, and Philadelphia. Many are alarmed by events such as the Boston Massacre and the Boston Tea Party. The Continental Congress has just met in Philadelphia to discuss the tensions between the colonies and Great Britain. Some people in Burlington, such as Mary and Robert Barton, wonder if the Patriots have gone too far. As Act I opens, the Barton family is sitting around the fireplace in their home. They are discussing what has been taking place in the colonies, as well as what these events mean for colonists like themselves.

Robert: Ben, did you see the big merchant ship in the harbor? Three masts! What a beauty! And she has brought us a new shipment of goods for the store.

Ben: Yes, Father. I watched them unload her. I kept wondering if the Patriots would sneak onto the ship and dump tea into the harbor as they did in Boston.

Mary: Ben, I don't think you will see that kind of tea party here in Burlington.

Robert: Well, Mary, I wouldn't be so sure. I spoke with your brother today. We're lucky that he works for the royal governor. Governor Franklin is a good man, but no doubt your brother is worried. It seems that some people are saying that we should not have a royal governor.

Mary: Oh, surely such talk will not amount to anything. William Franklin is a good governor. He has served the people of this colony well and deserves our respect. The governor simply supports King George, as he should.

Robert: That is true. He's loyal to Great Britain and has represented us well. But those rebels, the Patriots, call him a traitor.

Mary: He is not a traitor. It is the rebels who are traitors.

William: I don't know about that, Mother. I've heard talk amongst my friends. Some of the boys have been talking about the skirmish in Boston. Even though it happened a few years ago, the fight between the British soldiers and the Patriots has people upset. People call it the Boston Massacre.

Ben: Are you talking about how those British soldiers killed those people in Boston? I've wondered about that. Why *did* the soldiers shoot those men?

Robert: The shooting was a terrible mistake. Some boy threw a snowball at the British soldiers. In a panic, shots were fired. Unfortunately, those men died in what amounts to a tragic accident.

William: Yes, but why are troops here in Burlington now? We should not have British soldiers watching our every move. Some of my friends think that we, too, should be rebelling like the men in Boston.

Mary: The troops are here to defend the colonies, to protect us. It is absurd to talk about fighting the British Army. The British Army is the best and strongest in the world. Isn't that so, Robert?

Robert: Indeed. A bunch of farmers armed with pitchforks could never defeat the British Army. Besides,

British soldiers and those who are loyal to Britain greatly outnumber these rabble-rousers who call themselves Patriots.

Mary: The British soldiers make me feel safe.

Robert: As well they should. They are part of the strongest army in the world. We should be proud to be a part of Great Britain.

Ben: I like their red jackets.

William: Do they treat us like we are part of Great Britain? The Patriot leaders are meeting in Philadelphia to discuss this very point. After all, how much can we pay in taxes, Father? We have to buy stamps for paper, newspapers, and even playing cards, and some say that's just the beginning. And with all these taxes, do we get a say in the government? You'll see that more and more people are joining the Patriot cause.

Robert: How can you say that, William? Do not forget that Great Britain protected us against France in the last war! Wars cost a lot of money, and we should pay our part. Of course, I don't like to pay taxes any more than the next man. But it is our duty as subjects of the British crown.

Mary: Our taxes also pay for the soldiers who are stationed here to protect us. We can't expect Britain to send soldiers to the colonies for free. Someone has to pay their wages.

William: Some people say we should train our own soldiers to protect us.

Abigail: What about the women who say that they will not buy tea or cloth from Britain? Yesterday, I saw some women throw packages of tea out into the street, right in front of our store. And some of the women here in Burlington are setting up spinning groups to make their own cloth.

Mary: Those women are just foolish. Do not associate with any of them, Abigail. I forbid it. We are loyal to the king.

William: Not everyone is as loyal as you are, Mother. Many think that we should be able to govern ourselves. They say that we should not be taxed unless we have elected representatives to the British Parliament. Most important, they say we should stop trading with Great Britain and fight for our rights.

Robert: Stop trading? Well, that's simply absurd. Great Britain has goods we need. We have goods they need. It's simple. Both sides make money trading. A few wild-eyed rebels should not ruin our lives. Going to war with Britain would be foolish! The rebels would lose and then what would happen? No, war is not the answer!

Scene 2

In the Bartons' store

Narrator: Six months have passed. It is April 1775. Rebellion in the colonies has spread. Local farmers are refusing to sell their goods to Robert Barton and other Loyalists. William has been going to meetings of the Sons of Liberty, a vocal group of American colonists leading the independence movement. He and his friends have heard about Patrick Henry's famous "Give me liberty or give me death" speech, delivered in the Virginia House of Burgesses a month earlier. Some of his friends have joined the King's Regiment to support the British. The tension in the Barton family reflects the tense mood in the colonies. The scene opens as Robert and his children are waiting on customers at the Bartons' store.

Robert: William, could you help Mrs. Smith? I imagine she'll want her usual pound of tea. Is that right, Mrs. Smith?

Mrs. Smith: No tea today, Mr. Barton. I'm not buying tea. I have decided not to buy any more goods from Great Britain. Our taxes are just too high. I hear that you, Mr. Barton, are still loyal to the king. I don't understand that. But, in the meantime, I will have some vegetables from our local American farmers.

Robert: That is true, Mrs. Smith. I still support the king. I see no reason to change things here in America. So which vegetables would you like today?

William: Yes, how about these potatoes, Mrs. Smith?

Mrs. Smith: They look rather small compared to your usual produce. Is that the best you have?

Robert: I'm afraid so. Some of the farmers have refused to sell me their produce. They don't agree with my views about the colonies and Great Britain.

Mrs. Smith: Well, perhaps ... perhaps I should join them. You can keep the potatoes.

(Mrs. Smith exits the store.)

Abigail: My goodness, Mrs. Smith seemed quite bothered. What happened?

Robert: I regret to say that she has decided to stop buying goods from us.

Abigail: Why is that?

Robert: It seems she's become a rebel Patriot.

Abigail: Father, perhaps Mrs. Smith is right. Perhaps we shouldn't sell tea. Maybe we should sell only local produce—goods produced by people around here.

Robert: No, my dear. That is not my way. I have my beliefs and I will stand by them. I will not be forced to change my opinions.

William: Father, I think Abigail is right. And I think you should consider taking a loyalty oath—to the Patriot cause. Lots of people are doing it, you know. You don't have to support the **rebellion.** Just identify yourself with the Patriots.

Robert: William, we are loyal to the king, and that's final! Go out back and get some more tea. *Others* will want to buy it.

William: But, Father—

Robert: I will not let these so-called Patriots tell me what to do! *(A customer enters.)* Ah, Mr. Lawson, good day.

---

rebellion – an armed resistance against the government

Mr. Lawson: Good day, Robert. I'd like some cotton cloth and some tobacco.

Ben: And what about some tea, Mr. Lawson? It's just off the boat.

Mr. Lawson: Why, yes, tea would be nice, that's a good lad. I'm glad to see that you are stocking goods from Britain, Robert. I hear you cannot get a cup of tea in Boston. The rebels are trying to take over the city. But they'll have no luck. The British Army is there. Everyone knows there is no defeating a force that powerful.

Robert: I agree, Mr. Lawson. We have some fine cotton cloth that arrived on the same ship as the tea. I can give you a good price today.

Mr. Lawson: Excellent. I'll take eight yards. I'm proud to call myself a British subject, and I'm proud to buy British goods.

Robert: And I'm proud to sell them to you, Mr. Lawson. You have a good day, sir. *(Lawson exits.)* You see, children, there are still loyal citizens here in Burlington.

Ben: Father, what is that noise? *(Glancing out the window)* Look! An army of people is coming down the street.

William: They are carrying guns and pitchforks. They look like they're angry about something.

Robert: I know those men. They're farmers and townsmen. Why are they marching?

William: They're Patriots, Father, and they are coming toward our store!

Robert: Abigail, get in the back and take Ben with you.

William: Should I lock the door?

Robert: No! I have known most of those men for years! I'm sure that any issue they have can be discussed in a civilized manner. Surely they are just overexcited.

Scene 3

Outside the Bartons' store

Narrator: It seems that there's no time left for debate. Everyone has chosen sides. In New Jersey, people have been swearing allegiance to the independence movement by taking loyalty oaths. The situation is growing tense and even dangerous. Those who refuse to take the oath could be tarred and feathered. This means that hot, sticky tar is poured over them. Then feathers are thrown on to humiliate them further. If they don't die from the scorching tar, they are severely burned. As the scene opens, a crowd of Patriots is approaching the Barton store. The crowd members want to take the law into their own hands. They want to judge and pass sentence on Robert Barton, a **staunch** Loyalist. The crowd pushes into the store.

Crowd Member 1: Come with us, Mr. Barton! Your days of loyalty to Britain are now over.

Robert: What do you want with me? Since when is loyalty to Britain considered a crime?

Crowd Member 2: You know why we're here! We have come to ask you a simple question. Are you loyal to the king, or do you support the Patriot cause?

---

staunch – to be loyal and committed to an idea

Robert: My views and opinions are my own. I will not share them with the public. You have no power over me. Leave my shop this instant, or I'll send for the soldiers.

Crowd Member 2: I don't see any British soldiers here to protect you. Do you see any, men?

Crowd: No!

Robert: I'm not going anywhere, and I am not giving in to an unruly mob.

Crowd Member 3: Yes, you are. We outnumber you, Mr. Barton, and you will tell us what we want to know.

Robert: William! Come here please!

Crowd Member 4: So, Robert Barton, subject of Great Britain, how do you plead? Are you still loyal to the British crown?

Robert: I am. We have only one ruler here, and it is King George III.

Crowd Member 4: He is guilty as charged.

Crowd: Tar and feather the traitor! Tar and feathers for him! Get that tar good and hot.

William: *(Enter William with a gun.)* Leave my father alone! He's a good man. He has paid his taxes and given most of you credit in his store. He has stood by you in hard times. Leave him alone, or I'll be forced to use this gun.

(Enter shopkeepers and townspeople in a show of support.)

Shopkeeper 1: Stop it now! This is not the answer. Look, I'm a Patriot. All of you know that. I want us to be independent, but attacking Robert Barton will not solve our problems. Our issues are with Great Britain, not Robert Barton. We have no reason to quarrel with this man.

Shopkeeper 2: He's right. Attacking our neighbors won't win you any support. Mr. Barton has always been a good friend to us all. Stop and think about what you're doing. Leave him alone.

Crowd Member 5: But he is with Britain, not with us.

Shopkeeper 1: This is not a fair trial. This is an unruly mob. We are fighting for freedom and independence. In the name of freedom, let him go.

(The crowd starts to back down and several members slowly move towards the door.)

Crowd Member 5: You may have escaped this time, Barton, but your days in Burlington are numbered.

(The mob leaves.)

Robert: Let's go home now. But first, I think we'd better board up the store. Thank you, friends, and thank you, William, for standing up for me. That was very brave.

(The shopkeepers tip their hats to Robert and leave.)

William: No matter what sympathies I feel for the Patriots, I will always defend my family. I hope you know that, Father. I was really frightened, though.

Ben: I was frightened, too. I thought they were going to hurt you, Father.

Abigail: Oh, Father, what are we to do? It seems as if the whole town is against us.

Robert: We will carry on the best we can. We will get through this, don't worry. That crowd of men was frightening, but there are others in this town who are on our side. William, give me a hand with these boards. We need to cover up the windows.

Ben: I'll get the hammer and nails.

Abigail: I'll try to find Mother.

William: Father, these men are serious. Don't you think you should begin supporting the Patriot cause?

Robert: Never. A mob of angry rebels trying to threaten me has only made my beliefs stronger. I will not let a bunch of bullies tell me what I can and can't believe.

William: But your life may be in danger. And what if no one decides to shop in our store anymore?

Robert: If that is the way it has to be, then so be it. I would sooner live on the street than go against what I think is right.

Act II

The Setting

Burlington, New Jersey, 1776

Scene 1

In the Bartons' home at breakfast

Narrator: Tensions are running high in the Barton household. Mary and Robert continue to support the British crown, while William hopes the family will see the Patriots' side. On July 4, 1776, the colonies declared independence from Britain. The colonies are now officially at war with the mother country. The British have been forced out of Boston, but they control the city of New York. George Washington, the leader of the Patriot army, has not won any major battles. But the Patriots are not backing down. In New Jersey, the Patriots have placed the royal governor under house arrest and sent him to Connecticut. Though this was a major setback, the Loyalists think that the war will be over quickly. Large regiments of British soldiers are stationed near Burlington to keep order in the town.

Robert: I still cannot believe that the rebels have arrested the governor. Imagine! A leader forced from office by a mob. These are hard times. Have you heard anything more from your brother, Mary?

Mary: No, I haven't. His wife writes that when the governor was arrested, she and my brother fled to New York. She feels safe there. She suggests we think about going there, too. Loyalists there are free to say and do what they want. The British have secured the city.

Abigail: But why would we move? This is our home. We are safe here, are we not?

Mary: I don't want to move, but it may be wise to at least consider it.

Robert: We would be forced to give up our home and the store.

William: It's not safe anywhere now. People on both sides are turning on each other. Look at the damage to the store. They smashed the windows and turned over the barrels of pickles. And the farmers refuse to sell produce to Father.

Abigail: Those men had no right to damage our store. Our family has been nothing but kind to the people in this town.

Robert: That's true. People are not thinking straight. I don't see how the rebels can defeat the British Army. In the meantime, we'll just have to go about our business. There is no use worrying about something that hasn't even happened yet.

William: General Washington is leading the Continental Army, Father. He is a fine leader.

Robert: Well, he may be a fine leader, but he has not won any battles. Those rebel Patriots have no navy, and their army needs guns and supplies. They don't stand a chance!

William: I don't know about that, Father. The Patriots are a pretty determined bunch, and they're determined to govern themselves. Have you read *Common Sense?* Thomas Paine explains that Great Britain will continue to tax us until we have nothing left. Freedom will cost us, but *we will be free.*

Mary: Thomas Paine is nothing more than a troublemaker. People should have the common sense not to read his pamphlets.

Robert: I've heard much about the firebrand Patriots— Samuel Adams and Patrick Henry and that fellow Thomas Paine. Paine couldn't keep a job in England, so he came over here to stir up trouble. Speeches and pamphlets are fine, William, but soldiers win a war. Washington's ragtag band can never defeat the British.

William: You may be right, Father, but I think they're going to try.

Abigail: Most of our neighbors are joining the Patriot cause, Father. Women are knitting socks and scarves for the Continental Army. How can we not help? Why are we loyal to a country that is so far away?

Mary: Abigail Barton, what are you thinking? Your grandparents live in London, not Boston. We are British subjects.

Abigail: I know that, but many of the Patriots are our neighbors and friends.

William: We can't hide our heads in the sand, Mother. We have to stand up and speak out for what we believe in.

Mary: I am standing up for what I believe in, William. Your father and I believe in supporting the king.

Robert: Your mother is right, William, I cannot take that oath for the new government. Some may have declared themselves independent, but I have not.

William: I think you're making a terrible mistake. Obviously many others think so, too.

Robert: We've raised you to speak your mind, William. You may think I'm making a mistake, but I have to stand up for what I believe in.

Ben: If the Patriots win, I won't have to learn about the kings of Great Britain anymore!

William: No, instead you will learn about General George Washington and the other Patriot leaders.

Robert: Nonsense! Britain is a great country with a long tradition, and I want my children to learn about it and respect it. The rebels will not beat the British.

William: We shall see, Father.

Scene 2

In the Bartons' home and at
a Sons of Liberty meeting

Narrator: It is a cold winter night in December 1776. The wind is fierce, yet only two of the Bartons are asleep in their beds. In the dark, William quickly dresses and creeps down the back stairs. He is on his way to a meeting of the Sons of Liberty, which he has secretly joined. But before he can escape out the back door, Abigail and Ben stop him.

Divided Loyalties

Abigail: William, are you going to a Sons of Liberty meeting? You must take me with you!

William: Don't be silly, Abigail. Mother would be furious if she found out I had taken you to a meeting. And who knows what Father would do.

Ben: Then take me. I'll be good, I promise. I want to belong to the Sons of Liberty, too.

William: Look, you two, I need you to stay here in case Father wakes up. You have to cover for me.

Ben: Okay. I'll make sure no one notices you're missing. But I still wish I could go.

William: Go back to bed, Ben. You'll freeze in just your night shirt. And you know how angry Father will be if he finds you've left your bed.

Ben: Alright, I'm going. *(Ben exits.)*

Abigail: If you do not take me, William, I shall scream and wake up both Mother and Father.

William: Abigail, that is so unfair!

Abigail: I know it's unfair, but it's also unfair that I get left out. I want to be a Patriot as much as you do. I don't want to just knit socks like the other women.

William: Oh, come on, then. Dress warmly and hurry up.

Abigail: I'll be ready in five minutes!

Narrator: Abigail and William make their way through the night to the Sons of Liberty meeting. A soldier from Washington's army is there to recruit volunteers for the army. The time has come for Washington to move against the British Army. The Patriots know that if Washington doesn't win a victory soon, people will lose faith and the rebellion will be over. As Abigail and William arrive, the soldier is encouraging men in the group to join the Patriot army.

Soldier: General Washington needs some good men to help him. We need men to spy on the enemy soldiers and report on their movements, and we need men to join the army. I cannot share more information with you now, but know that this is important to our cause. Now who is with us?

Abigail: I can help.

Soldier: Thank you, miss, but we need soldiers.

Abigail: Women are fighting for your cause, too, sir. I can watch the soldiers and report their movements. Who will suspect a girl of gathering information?

Soldier: You make a good argument, young lady. Report your findings to Mr. Smith, the blacksmith. He is standing at the back of the room. And you, William Barton, what do you have to say for yourself? Remember what we are fighting for. It is our right to govern ourselves. We do not need Great Britain telling us how to live our lives. As Thomas Paine said, "These are the times that try men's souls." But if we work together and follow General Washington, we will find ourselves victorious.

William: I am ready to serve, sir. I can watch the soldiers and report back to you. And I am ready to join the Patriot army.

Soldier: Good man. Now who else will join the army and help us win our freedom?

Narrator: Abigail gets directions on how to pass on information about the British soldiers, and William receives a folded-up note from Mr. Smith. The meeting breaks up so that people can make it home before the British soldiers start their early morning patrols. William and Abigail race home, knowing that these desperate times are going to change their lives forever. When the roosters crow at dawn, Abigail and William are safely in their beds, but far too excited to sleep.

Scene 3

In the Bartons' living room

Narrator: It is a sad Christmas in the Barton house. Many Loyalist friends have left New Jersey for New York. Others are leaving for Great Britain or Canada. British ships have been **blockading** the harbors so that merchant ships can neither come in nor go out. The Barton's business has come to a standstill.

Washington has been forced out of New Jersey and waits across the Delaware River. It seems as though nothing is happening. But that is not the case. Both Abigail and William have been watching the soldiers and reporting their movements to Mr. Smith, who reports to the Patriot army. From these and other reports, Washington has been able to gain valuable information and form a plan. His plan is to prepare his soldiers early in the morning to surprise the British soldiers while they are sleeping. The scene opens as the Bartons exchange gifts on Christmas morning.

Robert: My dear family, I'm sorry for such a bleak Christmas. The British blockade of the harbor has nearly shut down our store. And, of course, the local farmers refuse to sell to me. So, we must be happy that we are all safe—and all here together.

---

blockade – to set up obstacles that make it impossible to pass

Abigail: Well, Father, for once no one will complain about my gifts. With the storm outside, we can all use the warm things that I've knitted.

Mary: You did a fine job, dear. Robert, my brother and his family are leaving New York for Great Britain. They will sail on the next ship. I hear that many other people are leaving during these difficult times.

Robert: Some are going to Canada for a fresh start. As we've already discovered, it's not easy being a Loyalist here.

Ben: I love my toy soldier! William carved one that looks like Washington.

William: I'm sorry it is only one. I have been busy these past few days.

Robert: Yes, where have you been going each night?

Abigail: Oh, Father, I love this piece of silk. How did you ever find it?

Mary: Your father went to the next town to find the silk for you. You can make yourself something nice with it. So, William, what have you been doing?

William: I have been meeting with friends, Mother. There is much to talk about these days. The truth is,

I have been attending Sons of Liberty meetings. I believe very strongly in the independence movement.

Robert: I'm quite disappointed, William, but I have raised you to think for yourself. I'm sorry that we don't see eye to eye.

Mary: Well, I'm more than disappointed. I am shocked that you have been meeting with those rebels and troublemakers.

William: I'm sorry you see me as a rebel, Mother. I think of myself as a Patriot, and I believe in this cause as much as you believe in yours.

Narrator: Later that evening, after the family is in bed, two of William's friends knock softly at the door. William is waiting on the stairs for them. Abigail sees them give William a Continental Army jacket and a gun. Her heart jumps, but she quickly hands William a note with the information she has collected about the soldiers' movements in and around Burlington. William disappears into the night.

William and his friends wait by the Delaware River with other men from Burlington. The winter storm has delayed Washington as he makes his way up the Delaware River, but it also helps him. The storm prevents the British soldiers from carrying out their early morning patrols. So Washington's army crosses the river unseen. William and his friends join the rest of the Patriot army when they arrive on shore. Washington's army surprises the British and quickly wins the Battle of Trenton. He captures more than nine hundred soldiers, their guns, and their supplies. The Patriots suffer only six casualties. The battle makes Washington a hero, and gives the Patriot cause new life.

(After the evening meal, the family is gathered near the fire.)

Mary: Abigail, where is your brother? Ben, have you seen William?

Ben: Mother, look at my toy soldiers all lined up to fight.

Mary: They are very brave, Ben.

Robert: I hope William isn't doing anything foolish.

(Suddenly William bursts into the house.)

Mary: William, where have you been? You're covered in mud! And you're carrying a gun! Is that a uniform?

William: I have been in a fight, Mother. I fought in the Battle of Trenton. And we won! Washington has won!

Robert: What do you mean? How could he defeat the British Army? There were more than a thousand men! Washington could not have won a battle that easily.

William: But he did, Father. We attacked early this morning. We crossed the river as soon as the storm let up. The British soldiers were still asleep. Washington had us surround them, and we cut off their escape routes. It's too late to tell me not to **enlist**.

Robert: I knew you were attending Sons of Liberty

---

enlist – to sign up or volunteer for military service

meetings, but now you are fighting with the rebels? William, are we to be enemies?

William: Never enemies, Father. We are still family.

Mary: William, you might have been killed.

William: But I wasn't, Mother. I am here, safe.

Robert: Yes, but for how long? No one who is fighting in battles is safe. How could you enlist?

William: It was a difficult decision, but we must be free of Great Britain. I think we can build a great new country.

Mary: Oh, William, I cannot believe you would betray us. Not like this, killing our countrymen in battle!

William: I have not betrayed you, Mother. We must all make grave sacrifices for our beliefs, British and Patriot alike. But one day we will all be better off, free from British control.

Robert: So, my son, this is the future then. The rebels have won you over.

Act III

The Setting

Burlington, New Jersey, 1777–1778

Scene 1

In the Bartons' living room

Narrator: It is now clear that the war will not end quickly. The Patriots, under General George Washington, have claimed victories at Trenton and Princeton. William continues to fight for them. In 1777, he is sent to Saratoga where he helps the Patriots win a major battle. Their continued success gives the Patriots more and more confidence. Many Loyalists are becoming discouraged. The British do, however, take Philadelphia, the capital of the new United States. But the Patriot leaders all escape. Washington's army encamps at Valley Forge in Pennsylvania for the winter. The British Army remains in New York.

It is a November evening in the Barton house in 1777. The family is gathered around the table, eating a modest dinner. William has returned from Saratoga to Burlington to visit his family now that the army is encamped for the winter at Valley Forge.

Mary: It's wonderful to have you here with us, William. Eat up, everyone. Abigail helped me make this broth. She is becoming a fine cook.

William: She is, and, with the blockade and the war, she does not have to worry about spices. There are none to be had.

Robert: With the mess you rebels have made of things, you should be thankful that we have food at all.

Ben: Well, I like Abigail's cooking.

Abigail: Thank you, Ben. You were quite a help. William, the vegetables are from Ben's garden.

Ben: I grew them myself.

Mary: We have had many meals made from your vegetables. You have become a good gardener.

William: Nice work, Ben. I'm very proud of you. Well, now that New Jersey is safely in the hands of the Patriots, perhaps we can get more supplies and food. General Washington is proving to be a great leader.

Robert: His luck does seem to be holding. I cannot believe that his army defeated us at Saratoga. But the British occupy Philadelphia. The Continental Congress had to flee the city. You can't respect a government that runs and hides.

William: The Congress
is still working hard,
Father. They are writing
laws that are fair, something
that Great Britain never did.
And our new flag now proudly
flies in battle.

Mary: Well, that flag will never fly in
this house.

Abigail: Must we all be on opposite sides?
The war should not divide our family.

Robert: Abigail is right. We may have different
views but we are still a family.

William: I agree, but we all must do what we feel is
right. I think we need to support this new country.
I believe that all men are created equal.

Abigail: And, as Mrs. Adams said, "Do not forget the
ladies." We women are making sacrifices, too.

Ben: What was it like to fight in the Battle of Saratoga,
William? Was it exciting?

William: Well, it was a lot of hiding in the woods. We
made surprise attacks when we could. And it was
really hot. The first battle was in mid-September and
we nearly beat them. But then soldiers came to

reinforce the British and they held us off. In the next battle, in October, we came charging out of the woods and we almost had them in the first hour. But they put up a good fight.

Ben: So were you scared? What did you do at night? Where did you sleep?

William: Well, we slept in tents under the stars on a bed of straw, and to bring ourselves comfort we sometimes sang and told stories. Often there was nothing for us to do but wait. It was lonely sometimes, too, and of course I feared for my life. But I knew our cause needed our strength.

Abigail: Did you stand in a line like the British Army and fire across a field at them?

William: Sometimes we did. And sometimes we fired the cannon at a whole line of soldiers coming at us and then fired our muskets after that.

Abigail: Oh, William, you are so brave. It's so exciting to know that you defeated the British Army.

William: Yes, it is exciting, but it's also terrible. I have seen many men killed on both sides.

Mary: William, you must promise me to look after yourself and to keep your head down.

William: I will, Mother, the best I can. People are saying it's the turning point of the war. Now Washington has an army of more than 20,000 men.

Robert: I cannot listen to this any longer! We have decisions to make. Children, please excuse your mother and me. We have to discuss our future.

Abigail: Father, we're all in this together. Please let us hear what you have to say, and then perhaps you could hear what we have to say.

Robert: We have raised you to think, so, yes, all right. We will share our bad news with you. As you know, the blockade has kept us from shipping or getting goods from Britain, and no one here will sell their goods to me. Before you say I should join the Patriot side, William, let me finish. I love our home, and I still care for our neighbors, but I also want us to be safe. The time has come. We must leave New Jersey and go to New York.

William: Must you leave, Father? Mother, you can't leave our home!

Mary: It is not what we want, William. We do not want to leave, but we must. It is not safe for Loyalists. And, no, we cannot change our views. You have chosen your cause, and we have chosen ours. We have friends in New York. Once we are there, we will decide on the next step.

Abigail: But what if we don't want to leave?

Robert: We have no choice, Abigail.

Scene 2

In the Bartons' store

Narrator: It is March 1778. The colonies have now become the United States of America. The Continental Congress has passed the Articles of Confederation to govern the new United States. All but one state, Maryland, has ratified the document. Still, the war rages on. Washington and his army are at Valley Forge. They are suffering in the cold, harsh winter while the British stay comfortable in New York. Many Loyalists have moved to New York, while others are selling their businesses and moving to either Canada or Great Britain.

The Bartons have made several important decisions. William has decided to leave his family and continue to fight in the Continental Army. Robert and the rest of his family have decided to make the journey to New

York. The scene opens as the Bartons sell the
remaining goods in the store and say goodbye to their
neighbors and friends.

Customer: So, you're letting the Patriots drive you out? I
had thought you would stay. Your son seems to find
the Patriot cause a righteous one.

Robert: William does what he believes, as do I. It is time
for the rest of us to move on.

Customer: Yes, it's better that you leave than be driven out of town as some have been. I remember you had a close call a few years ago.

Robert: Yes, it is not something I care to remember. Thank you for your business over the years.

Mary: Well, I have packed all that we can take with us, dear. There is nothing left for the rebels to steal.

Abigail: They wouldn't steal things from us, Mother. These are friends of William.

Ben: They stole from the other shops.

Robert: I am afraid Ben is right, Abigail. The rebels take what they need, and so do the British. Come, let us get home and finish packing. We must leave tomorrow.

William: So there is nothing that I can do to convince you to stay, Father?

Robert: No, William. We must leave.

William: You're making a mistake.

Robert: I think that *you* are making a mistake. You never would listen to reason. You always listen to your heart.

William: This time my head and my heart are telling me the same thing. I think it is you and Mother who will not listen to reason. It is clear the colonies must be free, and you are too stubborn to make the only reasonable decision. And you are dragging Abigail and Ben with you. Have you asked them how they feel and what they believe? They could have a future here in this new country. We all could!

Robert: William, I will not listen to your impudent and rash statements any longer! You are a traitor to all that I believe in. Get out of my house!

(William stares at his father, then exits.)

Abigail: Oh, Father, why did you have to argue? What if we never see William again?

Robert: That is the terrible price of war, Abigail.

Scene 3

At the dock

Narrator: It is early morning, and the Barton family, except for William, is gathered at the dock in Burlington. They are getting ready to board the ship that will take them to New York. Frantically, Abigail and Ben search for William in the crowd. Their distress is mirrored by the troubled looks of Robert

and Mary. The sadness of the moment weighs on all of them.

Robert: Come on now, let us move ahead. We must board the ship. We cannot miss it.

Abigail: Oh, please, Father, just a few more minutes.

Ben: Yes, we were hoping William would come to see us off.

Mary: I think he considers us the enemy now.

(Enter William.)

William: No, I don't, Mother. Ben, you look so grown up today.

Ben: William! I like your uniform!

Robert: So, William, you are still committed to the rebel Patriot cause, I see.

William: Yes, and I am still your son. I can help you if you stay.

Robert: No, we must leave. But I'm glad you've come. I'm sorry for what I said to you. You will always be my son. Here, take these keys. The house and the store are yours. They have served us well. You will have a business to come back to after the war.

Mary: We will send you letters there. I pray you stay safe. Remember we love you.

William: I'm a Patriot, Father, but I shall always love and respect you and Mother. I pray that we will all meet again in happier times.

(William watches them board. They wave from the deck.)

 Epilogue

Narrator: The Barton family went to New York and
then on to Canada. Abigail immediately began writing
to her brother. William fought in the war until it ended
in 1781. He was wounded, but not seriously. He
suffered more from the cold, the lack of food, and the
hardship of the winter months.

The family remained in Canada, and Robert
started a successful trading business. Abigail married
a Canadian merchant. After the Revolution she moved
back to America with her husband. She kept in touch
with her brother William. Ben stayed in Canada and
worked with his father.

William became a successful lawyer in New Jersey.
He married and lived in his old home in Burlington.
William saw his parents and Ben a few times after the
war. William and Abigail and their families kept in
touch throughout their lives.

The American Revolution

A New Country

On April 19, 1775, the American colonists went to war against Great Britain. Most people thought the war would end quickly. The Continental Army was not trained to fight. Most of the soldiers were farmers. The army had little money for uniforms or supplies, and their weapons were poor. In contrast, the British Army was very powerful. Its soldiers were well-trained. They used the finest weapons in battle. Yet despite the British advantage, the war lasted for more than six years. In the end, the colonists won. On October 17, 1781, the British Army surrendered at Yorktown, Virginia. The United States would become a new country.

The British surrendering at Yorktown

Opposite Beliefs

American colonists were forced to choose sides during the war.

Loyalists were colonists who believed that the colonies should remain part of Great Britain.

Patriots were colonists who believed the colonies should be independent from Great Britain.

Loyalists and the War

Loyalists traveling to Canada

Loyalists did not have an easy time during the war. Laws were passed against them. In some areas, Loyalists were not allowed to vote. Others had property taken away. Many Loyalists decided to leave the American colonies. After the war, the laws against Loyalists were removed. Over time, Loyalists living in the United States were accepted in the new country, and they became proud citizens.

Patriots and the War

Many people were surprised that the colonists could win a war against Great Britain. But after six years of battle, the British were defeated. After their victory, many Patriots became leaders in the new country. George Washington commanded the Continental Army. After the war, he became the first president of the United States. Other Patriot officers and generals became members of Congress.

President George Washington

Write a Newspaper Article

Imagine the year is 1774. You are a newspaper reporter assigned to explain reasons for the tension in the colonies.

- Copy the chart shown below into your notebook.

- In the left column, list three historical events discussed in the story or the timeline, in the order they occurred.

- In the second column, list information about each event.

- Use the information from the story and other resources to complete your chart.

- Then write your article. Use dates and clue words such as *first*, *next*, *then*, and *last* to show the sequence of the events.

Event	Information about the event
1. The Boston Massacre	British soldiers shot at townspeople. Five townspeople died. Soldiers were supposed to protect the people.
2.	
3.	

Read More About the American Revolution

Find and read more books about the American Revolution. As you read, think about these questions. They will help you understand more about this topic.

- How was colonial life different from life today?

- What events contributed to the tensions between the colonists and Great Britain?

- Why didn't Great Britain want the colonies to gain independence?

- Who were the men and women who helped gain American independence?

SUGGESTED READING
Reading Expeditions
People Who Changed America: Fight for Freedom

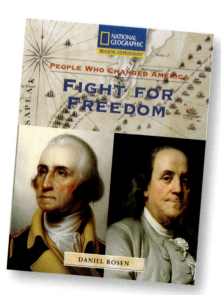